JEFFERSON COLLEGE

3 6021 00026 9

P9-CFH-763

MÊME MES CRITIQUES
RATENT
LA CIBLE

Jefferson College Library
Hillsboro, Mo. 63050

Charlie Brown et sa bande (9 titres de 128 pages chacun)

Charlie Brown (16 titres de 64 pages chacun, non disponibles aux États-Unis)

Charlie Brown et sa bande

MÊME MES CRITIQUES RATENT LA CIBLE

Traduit et adapté par Irène Lamarre

Holt, Rinehart and Winston / New York.

Les Éditions HRW ltée

Charles M. Schulz

MÊME MES CRITIQUES RATENT LA CIBLE

Copyright © 1981 by United Feature Syndicate, Inc.

PEANUTS comic strips from *DON'T HASSLE ME WITH YOUR SIGHS, CHUCK* (Copyright © 1975, 1976 by United Feature Syndicate, Inc.)

PEANUTS comic strips from *SUMMERS FLY, WINTERS WALK* (Copyright © 1976, 1977 by United Feature Syndicate, Inc.)

PEANUTS comic strips from *AND A WOODSTOCK IN A BIRCH TREE* (Copyright © 1978, 1979 by United Feature Syndicate, Inc.)

PEANUTS comic strips from *HERE COMES THE APRIL FOOL!* (Copyright © 1979, 1980 by United Feature Syndicate, Inc.)

Publié en 1981 par **Les Éditions HRW ltée**, Montréal.

Tous droits réservés.

Il est illégal de reproduire une partie quelconque de ce livre sans l'autorisation de la maison d'édition. La reproduction de cette publication, par n'importe quel procédé, sera considérée comme une violation du copyright.

Published simultaneously in the United States by Holt, Rinehart and Winston, 383 Madison Avenue, New York, New York 10017.

All rights reserved, including the right to reproduce this book or portions thereof in any form.

Library of Congress Catalog Card Number: 81-85103

ISBN (Canada): 0-03-926258-8
ISBN (U.S.A.): 0-03-061649-2

Dépôt légal 4e trimestre   Imprimé au Canada
Bibliothèque nationale du Québec   1 2 3 4 5 ML 85 84 83 82 81

Composition et montage: Ateliers de Typographie Collette inc.

PEANUTS comic strips to follow: © 1978 United Feature Syndicate, Inc.

VOICI QUELQUE CHOSE DE TOUT NOUVEAU...
C'EST UN SAVANT MÉLANGE D'OMELETTE ESPAGNOLE, DE SPAGHETTI ITALIEN, DE GOULASH HONGROISE ET DE CHARLOTTE RUSSE.
VOICI QUELQUE CHOSE DE TOUT NOUVEAU AUSSI...
J'AI PERDU L'APPÉTIT!
SCHULZ

HÉ, CHAT STUPIDE! NOUS AVONS EU UNE BONNE AVERSE LA NUIT DERNIÈRE, N'EST-CE PAS?
C'EST BON POUR LES FLEURS... ÉVIDEMMENT UN RUSTRE COMME TOI NE CONNAÎT RIEN AU FLEURS!
CRAAC!
SCHULZ

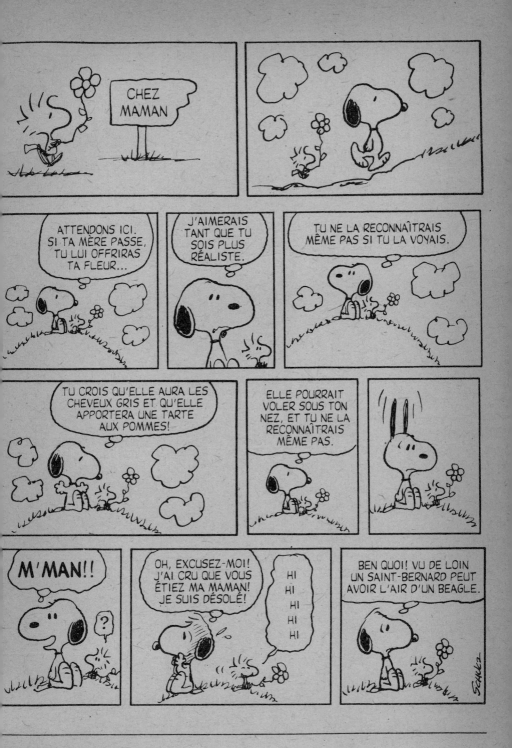

JE COMPRENDS POURQUOI TU AIMES TANT LE SOCCER, LUCIE...
LA COURSE... LE JEU DE PIEDS...
EN PLUS, C'EST UN VRAI JEU D'ÉQUIPE... RÉUSSIR UN BON COUP PEUT ÊTRE TRÈS GRATIFIANT...
J'AIME JUSTE FRAPPER SUR LES CHOSES.
SCHULZ

QU'EN DIS-TU? J'AI MARCHÉ DE LA MAISON À TA NICHE AVEC TON BOL SUR LA TÊTE!
C'EST CE QUI ARRIVE QUAND ON MANGE TROP SOUVENT AU MÊME ENDROIT!
SCHULZ

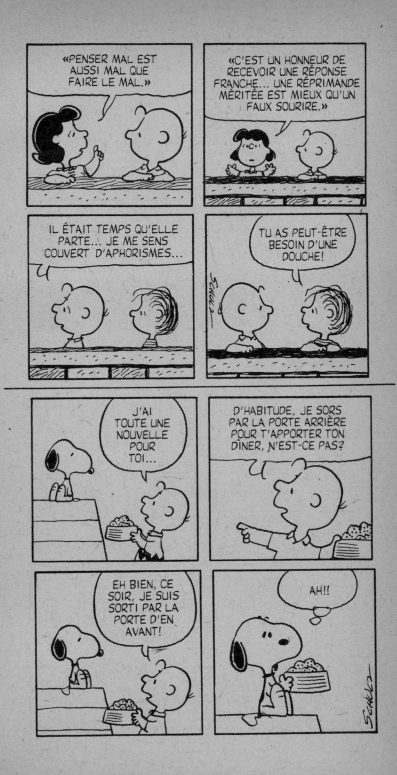

PEANUTS comic strips to follow: Copyright © 1979 by United Feature Syndicate, Inc.

Au départ, le cowboy tint sa monture à fond de train.
Il dut cependant bientôt ralentir.
La région devenait de plus en plus
valllll!llonneuse.
SCHULZ

i i i i i i i i i
PLEURA LE CHIEN
i i i i i i i i i i i i
i i i i i i i i i i i i
i i i i i i i i i i i i i
i i i i i i i i i i i i i
MADA'AAME?
SI VOUS VOULEZ, MAIS L'EFFET SERA RATÉ!
SCHULZ

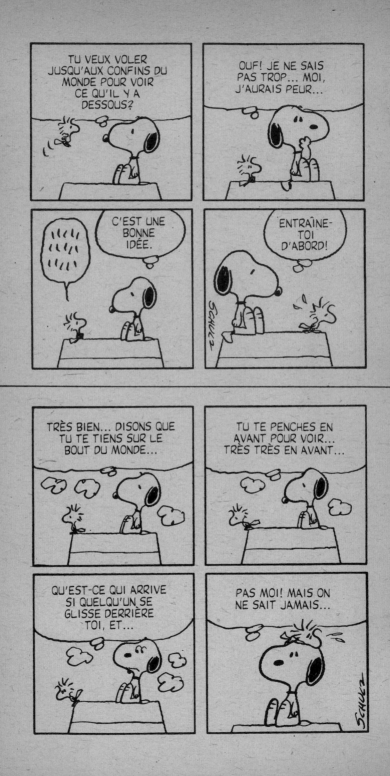

PEANUTS comic strips to follow: Copyright © 1980 by United Feature Syndicate, Inc.